KS2
7–8
Years

Master Maths at Home

Measuring

Scan the QR code to help your child's learning at home.

DK | MATHS NO PROBLEM!

mastermathsathome.com

How to use this book

Maths — No Problem! created **Master Maths at Home** to help children develop fluency in the subject and a rich understanding of core concepts.

Key features of the Master Maths at Home books include:

- Carefully designed lessons that provide structure, but also allow flexibility in how they're used.

- Speech bubbles containing content designed to spark diverse conversations, with many discussion points that don't have obvious 'right' or 'wrong' answers.

- Rich illustrations that will guide children to a discussion of shapes and units of measurement, allowing them to make connections to the wider world around them.

- Exercises that allow a flexible approach and can be adapted to suit any child's cognitive or functional ability.

- Clearly laid-out pages that encourage children to practise a range of higher-order skills.

- A community of friendly and relatable characters who introduce each lesson and come along as your child progresses through the series.

You can see more guidance on how to use these books at **mastermathsathome.com**.

We're excited to share all the ways you can learn maths!

Maths — No Problem!
mastermathsathome.com
www.mathsnoproblem.com
hello@mathsnoproblem.com

First published in Great Britain in 2022 by
Dorling Kindersley Limited
One Embassy Gardens, 8 Viaduct Gardens, London SW11 7BW
A Penguin Random House Company

The authorised representative in the EEA is Dorling Kindersley
Verlag GmbH. Amulfstr. 124, 80636 Munich, Germany

10 9 8 7 6 5 4 3 2 1
001–327084–Jan/22

A CIP catalogue record for this book is available from the British Library.

ISBN: 978-0-24153-926-2
Printed and bound in the UK

For the curious
www.dk.com

MIX
Paper from
responsible sources
FSC™ C018179

This book was made with Forest Stewardship Council™ certified paper - one small step in DK's commitment to a sustainable future. For more information go to www.dk.com/our-green-pledge

Acknowledgements
The publisher would like to thank the authors and consultants Andy Psarianos, Judy Hornigold, Adam Gifford and Dr Anne Hermanson.

The Castledown typeface has been used with permission from the Colophon Foundry.

Contents

Ruby   Elliott   Amira   Charles   Lulu   Sam   Oak   Holly   Ravi   Emma   Jacob   Hannah

Measuring in metres and centimetres

Starter

How tall is the sunflower?

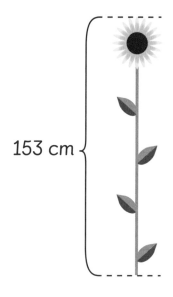

153 cm

Example

We can use a tape measure to measure the height and length of objects.

We can measure objects in metres and centimetres.

We write metres as m.

We write centimetres as cm.

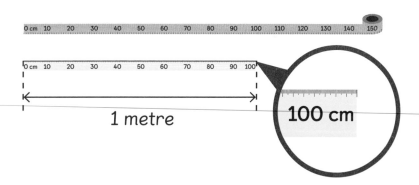

1 metre

100 cm

4

The height of the sunflower is 1 m 53 cm.

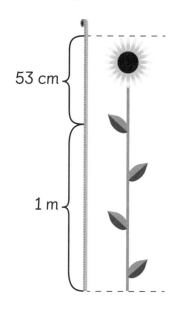

53 cm

1 m

1 m 53 cm

100 cm or 1 m

53 cm

153 cm

1 m 53 cm = 100 cm + 53 cm = 153 cm

Practice

1 Write the height of the street light in metres and centimetres.

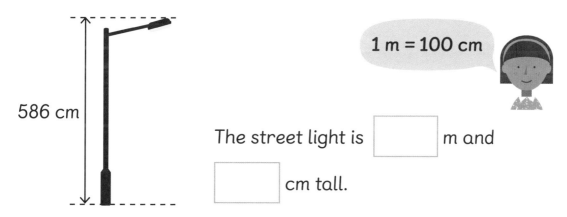

586 cm

1 m = 100 cm

The street light is [ ] m and

[ ] cm tall.

2 Fill in the blanks.

(a) 1 m 43 cm = [ ] cm

(b) [ ] m [ ] cm = 210 cm

(c) 5 m 15 cm = [ ] cm

(d) [ ] m [ ] cm = 307 cm

(e) 1 m 1 cm = [ ] cm

Writing length in metres and kilometres

Starter

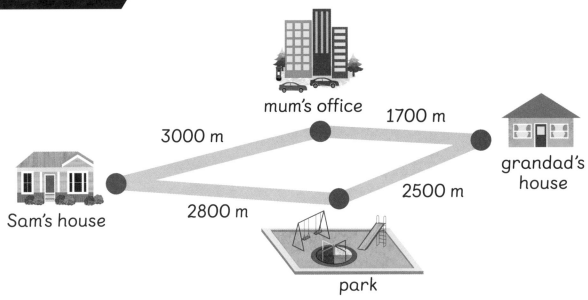

3000 m

mum's office

1700 m

Sam's house

2800 m

park

2500 m

grandad's house

How can we write these distances in kilometres and metres?

Example

The distance from Sam's house to the park is 2800 m.
2800 m = 2000 m + 800 m

2800 m = 2 km 800 m

1000 m = 1 km

2000 m or 2 km

2800 m

2 km 800 m

800 m

Practice

1 Write these distances in kilometres and metres.

Journey	Distance in m	Distance in km and m
Sam's house to mum's office	3000 m	
grandad's house to the park	2500 m	
grandad's house to mum's office	1700 m	

2 Find the total distance in kilometres and metres.

(a) Sam leaves his house, passes his mum's office and goes to his grandad's house.

☐ km ☐ m

(b) Sam leaves his house, passes the park and goes to his grandad's house.

☐ km ☐ m

3 Convert these distances into kilometres and metres.

(a) 3500 m = ☐ km ☐ m

(b) 2000 m = ☐ km ☐ m

(c) 1750 m = ☐ km ☐ m

(d) 900 m = ☐ km ☐ m

Comparing length

On Friday, Lulu walked from the information centre to the forest. On Saturday, she walked from the information centre to the hills. Which distance is longer?

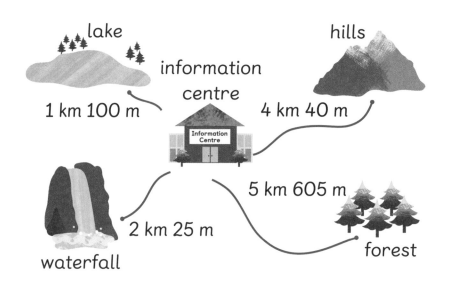

lake

information centre

hills

1 km 100 m

4 km 40 m

Information Centre

5 km 605 m

2 km 25 m

waterfall

forest

Example

We can write the distances in kilometres and metres. We can also write them using only metres.

1 km = 1000 m

Location	Distance from the information centre in km and m	Distance from the information centre in m
lake	1 km 100 m	1100 m
hills	4 km 40 m	4040 m
forest	5 km 605 m	5605 m
waterfall	2 km 25 m	2025 m

The distance from the information centre to the forest is 5 km 605 m or 5605 m.
The distance from the information centre to the hills is 4 km 40 m or 4040 m.

5605 > 4040
5605 m is greater than 4040 m.

The distance from the information centre to the forest is longer than the distance from the information centre to the hills.

1100 m, 2025 m, 4040 m, 5605 m

shortest ⟶ longest

We can order the distances from shortest to longest.

Practice

1 (a) Complete the table.

(b) Order the distances in metres from longest to shortest.

[_____] , [_____] ,

[_____] , [_____]

Distance in km and m	Distance in m
3 km 30 m	
5 km	
	1070 m
	3300 m

2 During the school holidays Amira and her family travelled to nearby attractions. On Monday they travelled 4 km 30 m to a beach. On Tuesday they travelled 5300 m to an adventure park. On Wednesday they travelled 430 m to a local farm.

(a) On which day did Amira and her family travel the longest distance?

[_____]

(b) Put the distances in order from longest to shortest.

[_____] , [_____] , [_____]

3 Emma and her friends measured their heights.

1 m = 100 cm

(a) Complete the table.

(b) Who is the tallest?

[_____]

(c) Who is the shortest?

[_____]

Name	Height in m and cm	Height in cm
Emma		113 cm
Elliott	1 m 35 cm	
Ravi	1 m 50 cm	
Ruby		110 cm

Reading weighing scales in grams

Which item is the heaviest? How can we be sure?

I think the bag of rice is the heaviest.

I think the bag of flour is the heaviest.

Example

Find the mass of each item.

 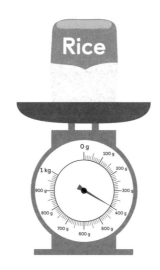 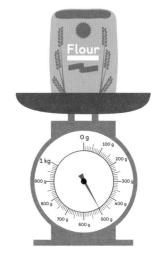

The packet of popcorn weighs 100 g.
It has a mass of 100 g.

The bag of rice weighs 400 g.
It has a mass of 400 g.

The bag of flour weighs 500 g.
It has a mass of 500 g.

The bag of flour is the heaviest.
The packet of popcorn is the lightest.

The bag of flour is 100 g heavier than the bag of rice.

Practice

Find the mass of each item in grams.

1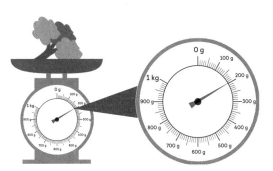

The broccoli weighs

☐ g.

2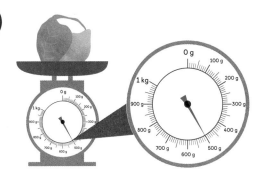

The cauliflower weighs

☐ g.

3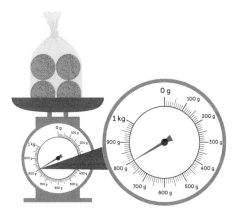

The mass of the bag of

oranges is ☐ g.

4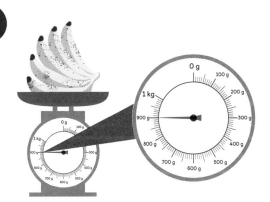

The bananas weigh ☐ g.

5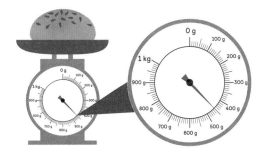

The mass of the loaf of

bread is ☐ g.

6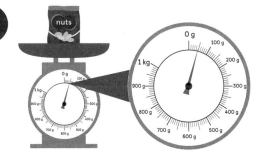

The packet of nuts weighs

☐ g.

Reading weighing scales in kilograms and grams

Starter

What is the mass of the parcel?

The weighing scales show the mass is between 3 kg and 4 kg.

Example

The weighing scales are marked in intervals of 200 g.

The parcel has a mass of more than 3 kg.
The mass of the parcel is 3 kg and 600 g.
We can write this as 3 kg 600 g or 3600 g.

1 kg = 1000 g

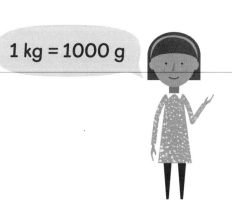

1 How much does each item weigh?

(a)

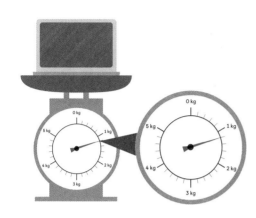

The laptop weighs

[ ] kg [ ] g.

(b)

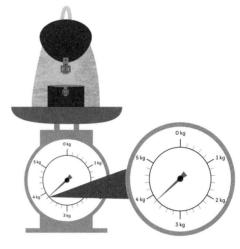

The backpack weighs

[ ] kg [ ] g.

2 Fill in the blanks.

(a) 3 kg = [ ] g

(b) [ ] kg = 5000 g

(c) [ ] kg [ ] g = 3300 g

(d) 3 kg 30 g = [ ] g

(e) [ ] kg [ ] g = 4750 g

3 Put these masses in order from lightest to heaviest.

1 kg 900 g   1 kg 90 g   990 g   1 kg

[   ] , [   ] , [   ] , [   ]

lightest   heaviest

Measuring volume

What is the volume of orange juice in Holly's glass?

Example

We can use a measuring jug to find out the volume of orange juice in Holly's glass.
The jug measures the volume of the liquid in millilitres.

We measure small volumes in millilitres (ml).

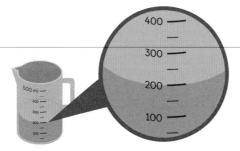

Volume is the amount of liquid in a container.

The volume of orange juice in Holly's glass is 200 ml.

Find the volume of water in each jug.

1

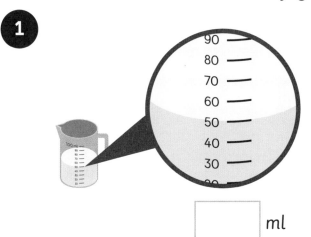

☐ ml

2

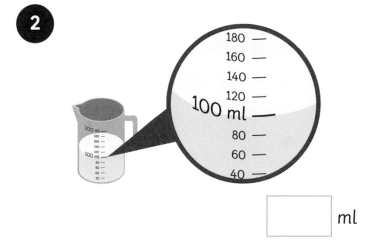

☐ ml

3

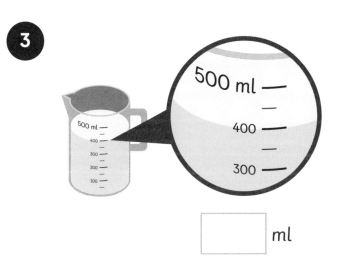

☐ ml

4

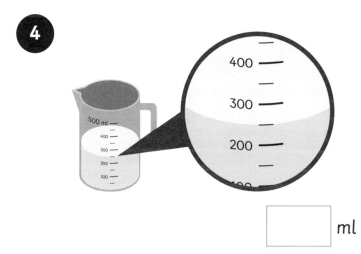

☐ ml

5

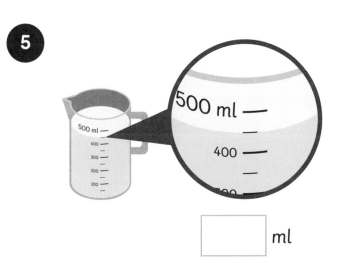

☐ ml

6

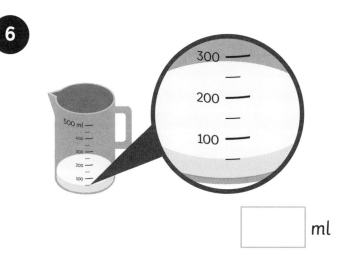

☐ ml

Measuring capacity

Which bottle holds the greatest amount of water?

How can we find out?

Example

The **capacity** of each bottle is how much liquid it can hold.
We can fill each bottle with water and empty it into a measuring jug.
The measuring jugs show the capacity of the bottles.

The has a capacity of 300 ml.

The has a capacity of 500 ml.

The has a capacity of 450 ml.

The bottle with the greatest capacity is .

The containers have been emptied
into the measuring jugs.
Find the capacity of each container.

Each container was completely
full before being poured
into the jugs.

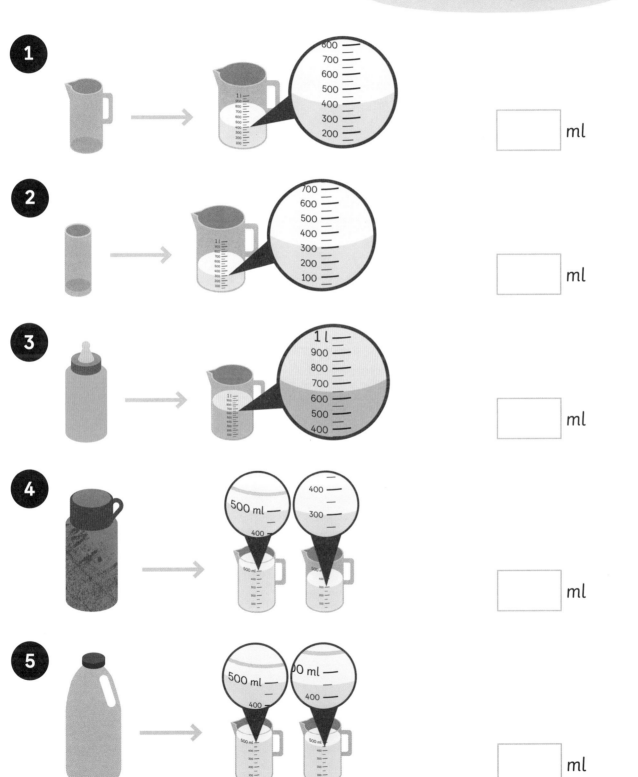

1

☐ ml

2

☐ ml

3

☐ ml

4

☐ ml

5

☐ ml

Comparing capacity

How can we compare the capacities of these containers?

Example

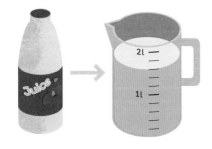  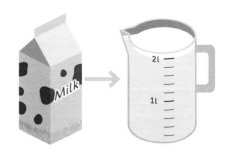

The  has a capacity of 1 l 600 ml or 1600 ml.

The  has a capacity of 1 l or 1000 ml.

The  has a capacity of 2 l or 2000 ml.

The  has the greatest capacity.

The  has the smallest capacity.

1 l = 1000 ml

18

Practice

1 Fill in the blanks.

(a) 2 l 500 ml = [ ] ml

(b) [ ] l = 3000 ml

(c) 1 l 50 ml = [ ] ml

(d) 4 l 400 ml = [ ] ml

(e) [ ] l [ ] ml = 4040 ml

2 Compare the capacities of the containers using greater or smaller.

(a)

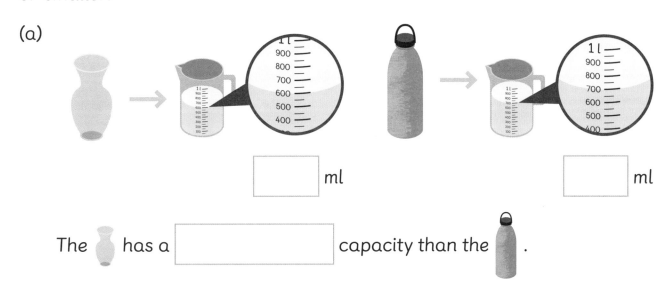

[ ] ml   [ ] ml

The 🏺 has a [ ] capacity than the 🍶 .

(b)

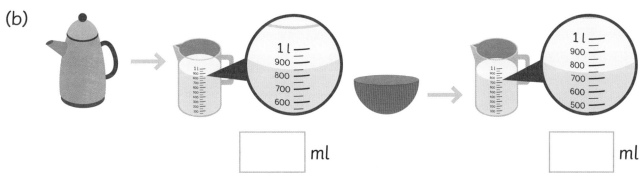

[ ] ml   [ ] ml

The 🫖 has a [ ] capacity than the 🥣 .

Adding money without renaming

Starter

Ravi has £16 and he wants to buy 2 items.

Which 2 items does Ravi have enough money to buy?

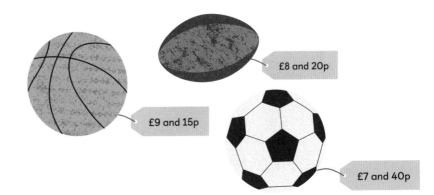

£8 and 20p

£9 and 15p

£7 and 40p

Example

Find the total price of and .

40p + 20p = 60p
£7 + £8 = £15

Add the pence and pounds together.

The total price of the 2 items is £15 and 60p.

 First we add the pence.

 We add the pounds next.

Find the total price of and .

15p + 40p = 55p
£9 + £7 = £16

The total price of the 2 items is £16 and 55p.

Find the total price of and .

15p + 20p = 35p
£9 + £8 = £17

The total price of the 2 items is £17 and 35p.

Ravi has enough money to buy and .

Practice

1 What is the total cost of each of the 2 items?

(a)

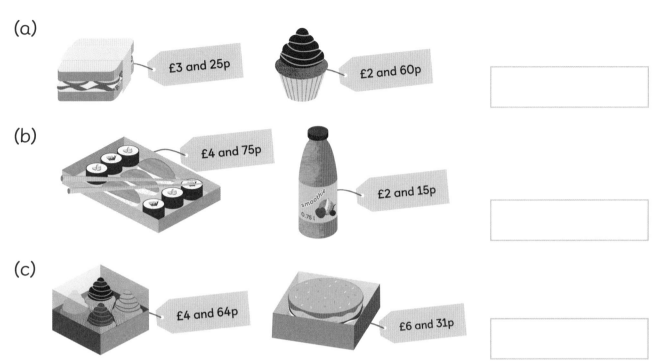

£3 and 25p

£2 and 60p

(b)

£4 and 75p

£2 and 15p

smoothie
0.75 l

(c)

£4 and 64p

£6 and 31p

2

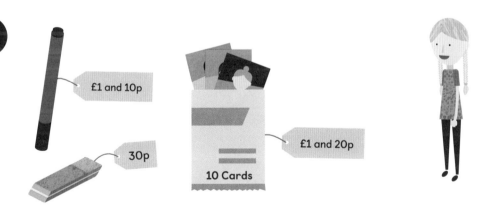

£1 and 10p

30p

£1 and 20p

10 Cards

(a) Hannah pays [ ] to buy 2 pens and a rubber.

(b) The total cost of a packet of cards and a pen is [ ].

(c) The total cost of the 3 items is [ ].

(d) Hannah spends £1 and 80p exactly. What does she buy?

[ ]

Adding money with renaming

Starter

 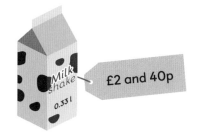

What is the total cost of Emma's lunch?

Example

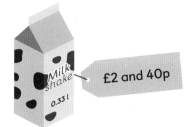

50 + 20 + 20 + 10 = £1

Add the pence.   90p + 40p = 130p

130p = £1 and 30p

Add the pounds.   £3 + £2 + £1 = £6

Add the pounds and the pence together.

The total cost of Emma's lunch is £6 and 30p.

Practice

1 Charles, Ravi and Holly bought the following items.
Find the total cost of each of the 2 items they bought.

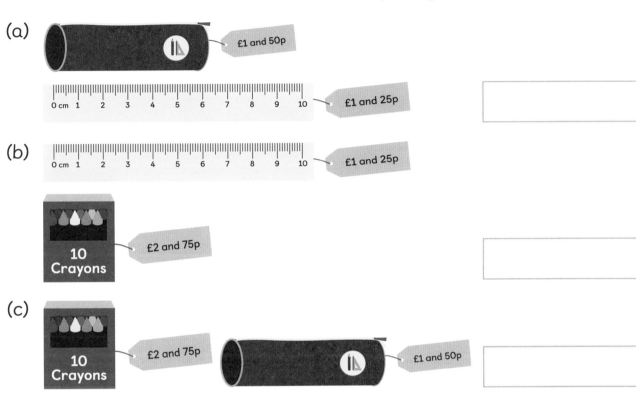

(a) £1 and 50p

£1 and 25p

(b) £1 and 25p

£2 and 75p

(c) £2 and 75p   £1 and 50p

2

£32 and 80p

£24 and 75p

£18 and 50p

(a) Lulu pays ⬜ for a tennis racket and a pair of
roller skates.

(b) Elliott spends £43 and 25p. What does he buy?

(c) Find the total cost of the 3 items. ⬜

Subtracting money without renaming

Starter

What is the price of the car in the sale?

sale! £1 and 50p off everything!!!

£9 and 75p

Example

Subtract the pence.
75p – 50p = 25p

Subtract the pounds.
£9 – £1 = £8

The price of the car in the sale is £8 and 25p.

Subtract £1 and 50p from £9 and 75p.

Practice

1 Find the sale price of the items.

sale! £1 and 50p
off
everything!!!

Take £1 and 50p off the items to find the sale price.

(a)

£5 and 60p

£2 £2 £1 50 10

The sale price is £ [ ] and [ ] p.

(b)

board game £8 and 95p

The sale price is £ [ ] and [ ] p.

(c)

£23 and 99p

The sale price is £ [ ] and [ ] p.

2 Subtract:

(a) £11 and 35p from £24 and 85p.

[ ]

(b) £14 and 17p from £68 and 89p.

[ ]

(c) £40 and 55p from £100 and 90p.

[ ]

Subtracting money with renaming

Starter

How much cheaper is the toy pyramid than the calculator?

£6 and 90p

£8 and 30p

Example

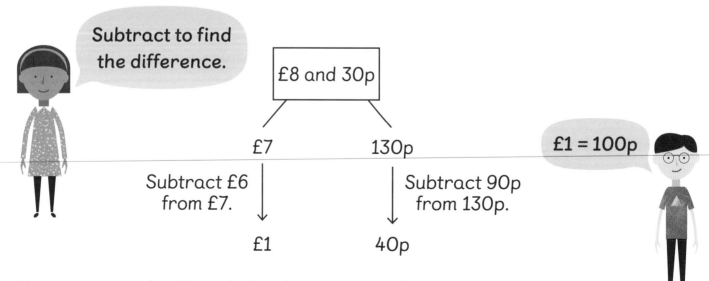

Subtract to find the difference.

£8 and 30p

£7   130p

£1 = 100p

Subtract £6 from £7.

Subtract 90p from 130p.

£1   40p

The toy pyramid is £1 and 40p cheaper than the calculator.

1   Find the difference in price between these items.

(a)

£3 and 40p   £1 and 80p

[ ]

(b)

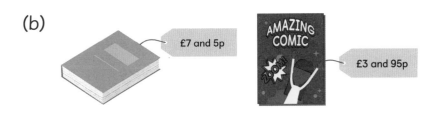

£7 and 5p   AMAZING COMIC   £3 and 95p

[ ]

(c)

£28 and 20p

£14 and 50p

[ ]

2

£43 and 60p

£32 and 85p

(a) Which item is cheaper? [ ]

(b) How much cheaper is it? [ ]

Adding and subtracting money

Starter

Hannah buys both of these posters.

£14 and 80p

£20 and 40p

How much change does she receive?

Example

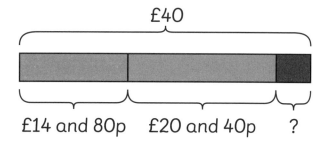

£40

£14 and 80p   £20 and 40p   ?

Add the pence.
80p + 40p = £1 and 20p

Add the pounds.
£14 + £20 = £34

Add the totals.
£34 + £1 and 20p = £35 and 20p

Subtract the total cost from £40.
£36 − £35 and 20p = 80p
£4 + 80p = £4 and 80p

Hannah receives £4 and 80p change.

 First we need to add the cost of the 2 posters to find the total cost.

 Hannah has £40. Next we need to subtract the total cost from £40.

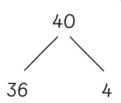

40
36   4

1 Ravi bought a pair of socks for £6 and 70p and a cap for £9 and 80p. He paid for the items with a £20 note. How much change did Ravi receive?

£20

£6 and 70p   £9 and 80p   ?

Ravi received £ [ ] and [ ] p change.

2 Holly bought a sweater for £21 and 20p and a scarf for £13 and 90p. She paid for the sweater and scarf using a £50 note. How much change did the shopkeeper give back to Holly?

The shopkeeper gave Holly back [ ] .

Telling the time to the minute

What time is it?

Example

Look at the minute hand on the clock.

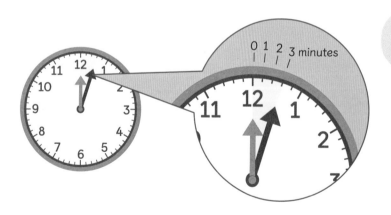

Each small mark on the clock represents 1 minute.

The minute hand is 3 minutes past the hour.

3 minutes past 12 is 12:03.

Practice

1 What time do the clocks show?

(a)

(b)

(c)

(d)

(e)

(f)

2 Draw the minute hand to show the following times.

(a)

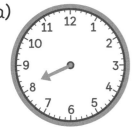

8:15

(b)

3:20

(c)

7:43

(d)

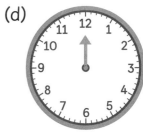

12:00

Telling the time on a digital clock

Starter

Is it 10:00 in the morning or 10:00 in the evening?

We say it is 10 o'clock in the morning.

Example

This is an analogue clock. It does not tell us whether it is a.m. or p.m.

A digital clock tells us if it is a.m. or p.m.

AM is the time between midnight and midday.

PM is the time between midday and midnight.

Practice

1 Draw the missing hands and fill in the blanks on the clocks.

(a)

11: ☐ ☐

(b)

07:45 ☐

(c)

☐ : ☐ ☐

2 What is the time?

(a)

07:10 am   10 past 7 in the morning

(b)

09:50 am   ☐ minutes to ☐ in the ☐

(c)

11:23 pm   ☐ minutes past ☐ at ☐

(d)

04:50 pm   ☐ minutes to ☐ in the ☐

Telling the time on a 24-hour clock

What time is it?

13:30

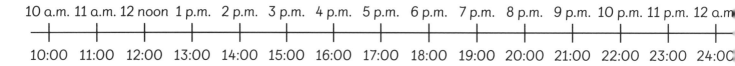

10 a.m.	11 a.m.	12 noon	1 p.m.	2 p.m.	3 p.m.	4 p.m.	5 p.m.	6 p.m.	7 p.m.	8 p.m.	9 p.m.	10 p.m.	11 p.m.	12 a.m
10:00	11:00	12:00	13:00	14:00	15:00	16:00	17:00	18:00	19:00	20:00	21:00	22:00	23:00	24:00

11:30   The clock shows 11:30 in the morning.

12:30   The clock shows 12:30 in the afternoon.

13:30   The clock shows 1:30 in the afternoon.

13:30 is half past 1 in the afternoon.

1 Match.

14:00	quarter to 9 in the evening
16:15	2 o'clock in the afternoon
12:30	quarter past 4 in the afternoon
20:45	half past 12 in the afternoon

2 Write these times as 24-hour clock times.

(a) 10 minutes past 3 in the afternoon ___ : ___

(b) 20 minutes to 12 in the morning ___ : ___

(c) half past 10 at night ___ : ___

(d) six thirty in the morning ___ : ___

Measuring time in seconds

Starter

The children timed how long it took to tie their shoelaces.
How long did it take each of them?

Example

We can use a stopwatch to measure time in seconds.

It took Elliott 12 seconds
to tie his shoelaces.

We can use the timer on a mobile phone.

It took Ruby 15 seconds
to tie her shoelaces.

We can also use the second hand on a clock.

It took Charles 16 seconds to tie his shoelaces.

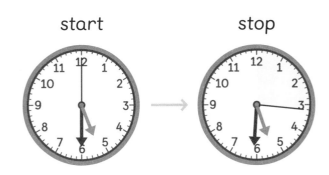

start   stop

1 Use a stopwatch or the timer on a mobile phone to time how long it takes to:

(a) sing Happy Birthday ⬚ seconds

(b) hop on one leg 10 times ⬚ seconds

(c) say the alphabet ⬚ seconds

2 How many seconds have passed?

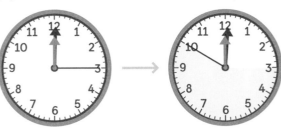

(a) start   stop

(b) start   stop

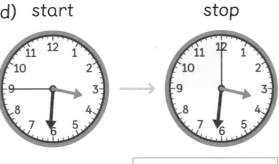

(c) start   stop

(d) start   stop

Measuring time in minutes and hours

Starter

For how long did Charles watch TV?

Example

Charles started watching TV at 5:30 p.m.
He finished watching TV at 6:15 p.m.

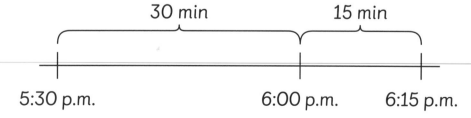

30 minutes + 15 minutes = 45 minutes

Charles watched TV for 45 minutes.

1 Holly started playing football at 6:20 p.m.
She finished at 7:10 p.m.
For how long did she play football?

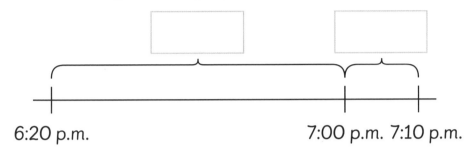

6:20 p.m.   7:00 p.m. 7:10 p.m.

Holly played football for [ ] minutes.

2 Ravi left home at 8:15 a.m. It took him 30 minutes to walk to school.
At what time did he arrive at school?

Ravi arrived at school at [ ] .

3 Find the end times.

start   end

(a)    →
        11:23   35 minutes later   [:]

(b)
        09:42   20 minutes later   [:]

Converting time

Starter

I took 125 seconds to solve the problem.

I took 2 minutes and 10 seconds to solve the problem.

Who took less time to solve the problem?

We can compare the times using minutes and seconds or using just seconds.

Example

Compare the times using minutes and seconds.

60 seconds = 1 minute
120 seconds = 2 minutes
125 seconds = 2 minutes 5 seconds

We write 2 minutes 5 seconds as 2 min 5 s.

Sam took 2 minutes 5 seconds.
Lulu took 2 minutes 10 seconds.

Compare the times using seconds.

2 minutes = 120 seconds

1 minute = 60 seconds

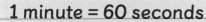

2 minutes 10 seconds = 130 seconds

Sam took 125 seconds.
Lulu took 130 seconds.

Sam took less time than Lulu to solve the problem.

1 Convert the following to seconds.

(a) 3 minutes ☐ seconds

(b) 2 minutes 25 seconds ☐ seconds

(c) 4 minutes 44 seconds ☐ seconds

2 Convert the following to minutes and seconds.

(a) 120 seconds ☐ minutes ☐ seconds

(b) 140 seconds ☐ minutes ☐ seconds

(c) 190 seconds ☐ minutes ☐ seconds

3 Holly took 165 seconds to make a smoothie.
Sam took 2 minutes 35 seconds to make a smoothie.
Who took longer to make a smoothie?

It took ☐ longer to make a smoothie.

4 Charles wanted to complete a level on his game in under 5 minutes.
He completed the level in 290 seconds.
Did he complete the level in under 5 minutes?

Review and challenge

1 Emma had 2 m of ribbon.
She made a bow with 75 cm of ribbon.
What length of ribbon did Emma have left over?

Emma had ☐ cm of ribbon left over.

2 Charles lives 3 km from school.
Hannah lives half the distance from the school that Charles does.
What is the distance Hannah lives from school?

school

Hannah's house

Charles's house

Hannah lives ☐ km ☐ m from school.

3 The dog weighs 500 g more than the cat weighs.
Find the mass of the dog.

2 kg 700 g

The mass of the dog is ☐ kg ☐ g.

4 Each week Mr Nightingale uses 200 ml of washing up liquid.
How many weeks will a full bottle of washing up liquid last
Mr Nightingale?

Washing
Up Liquid

1600 ml

A full bottle of washing up liquid will last Mr Nightingale

☐ weeks.

5 Find the total volume of water in the beakers.
Give your answer in litres and millilitres.

The total volume of water is ⬚ l ⬚ ml.

6 Ravi buys 👕 and 👖. He pays with a £50 note.

How much change does Ravi get?

£12 and 50p

£27 and 75p

Ravi gets ⬚ change.

7 Sam spent 2 hours and 30 minutes at a holiday club.
He left at 12 noon. At what time did he arrive?

9:00 a.m.	10:00 a.m.	11:00 a.m.		12 noon

Sam arrived at [ ] .

8 Lulu bought a dress for £28 and 75p and a coat for £32 and 55p.
She had £8 and 70p left after buying these two items.
How much money did she have to begin with?

Lulu had £ [ ] to begin with.

9 The mass of a box of 8 identical blocks is 900 g.
When 2 blocks are removed from the box, the mass of the box and remaining blocks is 720 g.
What is the mass of each block?

The mass of each block is [ ] g.

Answers

Page 5   **1** The street light is 5 m and 86 cm tall. **2 (a)** 1 m 43 cm = 143 cm **(b)** 2 m 10 cm = 210 cm
(c) 5 m 15 cm = 515 cm **(d)** 3 m 7 cm = 307 cm **(e)** 1 m 1 cm = 101 cm

Page 7   **1**

Journey	Distance in m	Distance in km and m
Sam's house to mum's office	3000 m	3 km
grandad's house to the park	2500 m	2 km 500 m
grandad's house to mum's office	1700 m	1 km 700 m

2 (a) 4 km 700 m **(b)** 5 km 300 m **3 (a)** 3500 m = 3 km 500 m **(b)** 2000 m = 2 km
(c) 1750 m = 1 km 750 m **(d)** 900 m = 900 m

Page 9   **1 (a)**

Distance in km and m	Distance in m
3 km 30 m	3030 m
5 km	5000 m
1 km 70 m	1070 m
3 km 300 m	3300 m

(b) 5000 m, 3300 m, 3030 m, 1070 m

2 (a) Tuesday **(b)** 5300 m, 4 km 30 m, 430 m

3 (a)

Name	Height in m and cm	Height in cm
Emma	1 m 13 cm	113 cm
Elliott	1 m 35 cm	135 cm
Ravi	1 m 50 cm	150 cm
Ruby	1 m 10 cm	110 cm

(b) Ravi **(c)** Ruby

Page 11   **1** The broccoli weighs 200 g. **2** The cauliflower weighs 500 g.
3 The mass of the bag of oranges is 800 g. **4** The bananas weigh 900 g.
5 The mass of the loaf of bread is 450 g. **6** The packet of nuts weighs 50 g.

Page 13   **1 (a)** The laptop weighs 1 kg 200 g **(b)** The backpack weighs 3 kg 800 g
2 (a) 3 kg = 3000 g **(b)** 5 kg = 5000 g **(c)** 3 kg 300 g = 3300 g **(d)** 3 kg 30 g = 3030 g
(e) 4 kg 750 g = 4750 g **3** 990 g, 1 kg, 1 kg 90 g, 1 kg 900 g

Page 15   **1** 50 ml **2** 100 ml **3** 400 ml **4** 250 ml **5** 450 ml **6** 50 ml

Page 17   **1** 400 ml **2** 300 ml **3** 650 ml **4** 800 ml **5** 950 ml

Page 19   **1** 2 l 500 ml = 2500 ml **(b)** 3 l = 3000 ml **(c)** 1 l 50 ml = 1050 ml **(d)** 4 l 400 ml = 4400 ml

(e) 4 l 40 ml = 4040 ml **2 (a)** 600 ml, 700 ml; The 🏺 has a smaller capacity than the 🍶.

(b) 850 ml, 750 ml; The 🫖 has a greater capacity than the 🥣.

Page 21　**1 (a)** £5 and 85p **(b)** £6 and 90p **(c)** £10 and 95p **2 (a)** Hannah pays £2 and 50p to buy 2 pens and a rubber. **(b)** The total cost of a packet of cards and a pen is £2 and 30p. **(c)** The total cost of the 3 items is £2 and 60p. **(d)** Hannah bought a packet of cards and 2 rubbers.

Page 23　**1 (a)** £2 and 75p **(b)** £4 **(c)** £4 and 25p **2 (a)** Lulu pays £57 and 55p for a tennis racket and a pair of roller skates. **(b)** Elliott buys a pair of roller skates and a bat. **(c)** £76 and 5p

Page 25　**1 (a)** The sale price is £4 and 10p. **(b)** The sale price is £7 and 45p. **(c)** The sale price is £22 and 49p. **2 (a)** £13 and 50p **(b)** £54 and 72p **(c)** £60 and 35p

Page 27　**1 (a)** £1 and 60p **(b)** £3 and 10p **(c)** £13 and 70p **2 (a)** The skateboard is cheaper. **(b)** It is £10 and 75p cheaper.

Page 29　**1** Ravi received £3 and 50p change. **2** The shopkeeper gave Holly back £14 and 90p.

Page 31　**1 (a)** 8:10 **(b)** 9:15 **(c)** 11:12 **(d)** 6:30 **(e)** 2:43 **(f)** 5:59

2 (a)　　　**(b)**　　　**(c)**　　　**(d)**

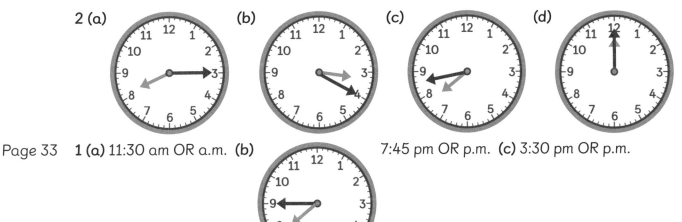

Page 33　**1 (a)** 11:30 am OR a.m. **(b)**　　　　　7:45 pm OR p.m. **(c)** 3:30 pm OR p.m.

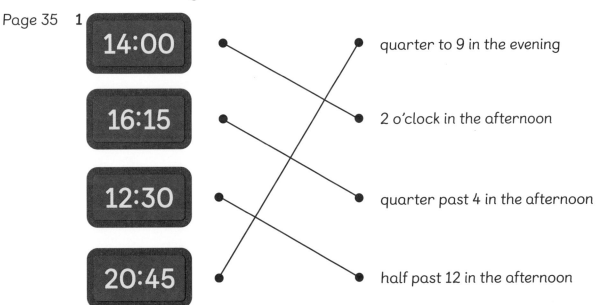

2 (b) 10 minutes to 10 in the morning **(c)** 23 minutes past 11 at night **(d)** 10 minutes to 5 in the morning

Page 35　**1**

14:00	→	quarter to 9 in the evening
16:15		2 o'clock in the afternoon
12:30		quarter past 4 in the afternoon
20:45		half past 12 in the afternoon

Answers continued

2 (a) 15:10 **(b)** 11:40 **(c)** 22:30 **(d)** 06:30

Page 37 **1 (a–c)** Answers will vary. **2 (a)** 20 seconds **(b)** 30 seconds **(c)** 35 seconds **(d)** 15 seconds

Page 39 **1** 40 min, 10 min; Holly played football for 50 minutes. **2** Ravi arrived at school at 8:45 a.m.
3 (a) 11:58 **(b)** 10:02

Page 41 **1 (a)** 180 seconds **(b)** 145 seconds **(c)** 284 seconds **2 (a)** 2 minutes **(b)** 2 minutes
20 seconds **(c)** 3 minutes 10 seconds **3** It took Holly longer to make a smoothie. **4** Yes

Page 42 **1** Emma had 125 cm of ribbon left over. **2** Hannah lives 1 km 500 m from school.

Page 43 **3** The mass of the dog is 3 kg 200 g. **4** A full bottle of washing up liquid will last
Mr Nightingale 8 weeks.

Page 44 **5** The total volume of water is 1 l 100 ml. **6** Ravi gets £9 and 75p change.

Page 45 **7** Sam arrived at 9:30 a.m. **8** Lulu had £70 to begin with. **9** The mass of each block is 90 g.

£6 and 90p

£8 and 30p

48